———— This Fashionista's Travel Diary Belongs to: ————

I always decide what travel style is; I don't follow others; I follow my gut.

~Kinyatta E. Gray

2022

JANUARY
S	M	T	W	T	F	S
						1
2	3	4	5	6	7	8
9	10	11	12	13	14	15
16	17	18	19	20	21	22
23	24	25	26	27	28	29
30	31					

FEBRUARY
S	M	T	W	T	F	S
		1	2	3	4	5
6	7	8	9	10	11	12
13	14	15	16	17	18	19
20	21	22	23	24	25	26
27	28					

MARCH
S	M	T	W	T	F	S
		1	2	3	4	5
6	7	8	9	10	11	12
13	14	15	16	17	18	19
20	21	22	23	24	25	26
27	28	29	30	31		

APRIL
S	M	T	W	T	F	S
					1	2
3	4	5	6	7	8	9
10	11	12	13	14	15	16
17	18	19	20	21	22	23
24	25	26	27	28	29	30

MAY
S	M	T	W	T	F	S
1	2	3	4	5	6	7
8	9	10	11	12	13	14
15	16	17	18	19	20	21
22	23	24	25	26	27	28
29	30	31				

JUNE
S	M	T	W	T	F	S
			1	2	3	4
5	6	7	8	9	10	11
12	13	14	15	16	17	18
19	20	21	22	23	24	25
26	27	28	29	30		

JULY
S	M	T	W	T	F	S
					1	2
3	4	5	6	7	8	9
10	11	12	13	14	15	16
17	18	19	20	21	22	23
24	25	26	27	28	29	30
31						

AUGUST
S	M	T	W	T	F	S
	1	2	3	4	5	6
7	8	9	10	11	12	13
14	15	16	17	18	19	20
21	22	23	24	25	26	27
28	29	30	31			

SEPTEMBER
S	M	T	W	T	F	S
				1	2	3
4	5	6	7	8	9	10
11	12	13	14	15	16	17
18	19	20	21	22	23	24
25	26	27	28	29	30	

OCTOBER
S	M	T	W	T	F	S
						1
2	3	4	5	6	7	8
9	10	11	12	13	14	15
16	17	18	19	20	21	22
23	24	25	26	27	28	29
30	31					

NOVEMBER
S	M	T	W	T	F	S
		1	2	3	4	5
6	7	8	9	10	11	12
13	14	15	16	17	18	19
20	21	22	23	24	25	26
27	28	29	30			

DECEMBER
S	M	T	W	T	F	S
				1	2	3
4	5	6	7	8	9	10
11	12	13	14	15	16	17
18	19	20	21	22	23	24
25	26	27	28	29	30	31

2023

JANUARY
S	M	T	W	T	F	S
1	2	3	4	5	6	7
8	9	10	11	12	13	14
15	16	17	18	19	20	21
22	23	24	25	26	27	28
29	30	31				

FEBRUARY
S	M	T	W	T	F	S
			1	2	3	4
5	6	7	8	9	10	11
12	13	14	15	16	17	18
19	20	21	22	23	24	25
26	27	28				

MARCH
S	M	T	W	T	F	S
			1	2	3	4
5	6	7	8	9	10	11
12	13	14	15	16	17	18
19	20	21	22	23	24	25
26	27	28	29	30	31	

APRIL
S	M	T	W	T	F	S
						1
2	3	4	5	6	7	8
9	10	11	12	13	14	15
16	17	18	19	20	21	22
23	24	25	26	27	28	29
30						

MAY
S	M	T	W	T	F	S
	1	2	3	4	5	6
7	8	9	10	11	12	13
14	15	16	17	18	19	20
21	22	23	24	25	26	27
28	29	30	31			

JUNE
S	M	T	W	T	F	S
				1	2	3
4	5	6	7	8	9	10
11	12	13	14	15	16	17
18	19	20	21	22	23	24
25	26	27	28	29	30	

JULY
S	M	T	W	T	F	S
						1
2	3	4	5	6	7	8
9	10	11	12	13	14	15
16	17	18	19	20	21	22
23	24	25	26	27	28	29
30	31					

AUGUST
S	M	T	W	T	F	S
		1	2	3	4	5
6	7	8	9	10	11	12
13	14	15	16	17	18	19
20	21	22	23	24	25	26
27	28	29	30	31		

SEPTEMBER
S	M	T	W	T	F	S
					1	2
3	4	5	6	7	8	9
10	11	12	13	14	15	16
17	18	19	20	21	22	23
24	25	26	27	28	29	30

OCTOBER
S	M	T	W	T	F	S
1	2	3	4	5	6	7
8	9	10	11	12	13	14
15	16	17	18	19	20	21
22	23	24	25	26	27	28
29	30	31				

NOVEMBER
S	M	T	W	T	F	S
			1	2	3	4
5	6	7	8	9	10	11
12	13	14	15	16	17	18
19	20	21	22	23	24	25
26	27	28	29	30		

DECEMBER
S	M	T	W	T	F	S
					1	2
3	4	5	6	7	8	9
10	11	12	13	14	15	16
17	18	19	20	21	22	23
24	25	26	27	28	29	30
31						

Fashionista's Travel Budget Planning

There are several things that all fashionistas need to think about when planning a fabulous vacation. Everything is going to revolve around your glam slam travel budget.

Your budget will drive the planning process. Don't mess this up! Consider these factors when planning your travel budget.

1. Think of your mode of travel (planes, trains, or automobiles). This is often the most expensive portion of your travel budget.
2. Think of where you will be staying. This will be the next big portion of your travel budget.
3. Think of how you will get around once you reach your destination. (Uber, rental car, taxi, horse and carriage, etc.)
4. Think of what you'll be eating. For example, will you stay in an accommodation with a mini kitchen and cook some meals, will you stay in an "All Inclusive" resort, or do you plan to eat out for every meal, every day, or will you have a cook and a butler?? Yes!!
5. Think of what you will be doing? Will you chill poolside during the trip soaking up the sun, or will you go parasailing and rock climbing. Will you visit the spa and totally relax during your vacation.
6. Think of emergencies. Anything could happen, and you'd want to have some extra cash and credit set aside in the event of an emergency.
7. Think of what you'll be buying. Are you really going to pass up that unforgettable handbag that you'll never see in the states? You can't travel without bringing your favorite relatives back their favorite duty-free liquor or that piece of furniture that you'll only see again in Africa!

Once you have assigned a dollar amount to all of these categories, you'll get a good idea of how much money you'll need to travel glam and fab!

Whether you work with a travel planner or planning a trip on your own, creating your travel budget and sticking to it is the way to go.

Fashionista Vacation Packing List

RESORT WEAR
- ☐ Tops
- ☐ Bottoms
- ☐ Sandals
- ☐ Beach/pool shoes
- ☐ Pumps/Dress shoes
- ☐ Swimsuits for each day
- ☐ Beach cover-ups
- ☐ Beach bag
- ☐ Beach hat
- ☐ Undergarments
- ☐ Sleepwear/silk scarf
- ☐ Light jacket
- ☐ Upscale Dinner Outfit w/small handbag

TRAVEL ESSENTIALS
- ☐ FlightsInStilettos Makeup Remover Facecloth
- ☐ FlightsInStilettos Face Mask
- ☐ FlightsInStilettos Glam Girl Beach Towels
- ☐ Makeup
- ☐ Nail polish
- ☐ Hair care products
- ☐ Ponytail Holders
- ☐ Bling headbands
- ☐ All essential toiletries
- ☐ Bar or liquid soap
- ☐ Sunscreen
- ☐ Lotion/body oil
- ☐ Mini first aid kit
- ☐ Prescriptions meds
- ☐ Shaving essentials
- ☐ Eyeglasses/Contact Lenses
- ☐ Hand sanitizer
- ☐ Costume jewelry or modest jewelry
- ☐ Sunshades

ENTERTAINMENT
- ☐ Fashion Magazines
- ☐ Books by Author Kinyatta E. Gray
- ☐ Mobile phone & charger
- ☐ Tablet & charger
- ☐ Ear buds

TRAVEL DOCUMENTS/ITINERARY
- ☐ Current passport for all travelers
- ☐ Travel Agent Business Card
- ☐ Cash/Credit Cards
- ☐ Photo ID
- ☐ Waterproof credit card holder
- ☐ Medical insurance card
- ☐ Travel insurance information
- ☐ Destination travel guide
- ☐ Ground transportation information
- ☐ Parking information at departure airport

BEFORE YOU LEAVE
- ☐ Make arrangements for pets or dependent family members who are not traveling
- ☐ Familiarize yourself with the destination's people, culture and language
- ☐ Check weather reports
- ☐ Water plants
- ☐ Set out garbage morning of travel
- ☐ Share travel itinerary with trusted friend/family member
- ☐ If traveling abroad register via Smart Traveler Program (Department of State)
- ☐ Submit hold request on mail if on extended travel
- ☐ Gas up your vehicle
- ☐ Take pics of credit cards/passport in case you lose them
- ☐ Check with airline for departure delays and information
- ☐ Set home alarm
- ☐ Ensure vehicles remaining home are locked
- ☐ Turn on porch lights
- ☐ Visualize everything going well!

7 Essential Rules for Glamorous Travel by FlightsInStilettos

1 **Start packing 6-months in advance.** This is necessary if you expect to remember everything you need to be the center of attention while on vacation. It takes time to order all of your shoes, your wardrobe, and accessories. It would be best if you had time to plan the perfect low maintenance - yet glam hairstyles for your vacation. For many of us, this involves hairpieces, braids, and wigs. You'll need time to order your FlightsInStilettos accessories or beach towels from **flightsinstilettos.com** when you're a glam traveler; the more lead time for packing, the better!

2 **Use a separate suitcase for EVERYTHING.** It doesn't matter that you're packing five suitcases for a weekend trip. What *does* matter is that you have everything you need while on your journey – because the worst thing that can happen is that you realize you packed the silver shoes, but you wanted the gold shoes! **So pack until you're content that every possible wardrobe and shoe combination/ option is available to you on your trip. In this case, more is better!**

3 **Bring ALL of your makeup.** This doesn't need any further explanation. Either you're glam, and you get it or not.

4 **Oversee the wardrobe, shoes, and accessories selections of your spouse or travel companion.** Your spouse or traveling companion's wardrobe, shoes, and accessories must compliment yours. Your travel companion can't possibly walk around with beat-up sneakers, «DAD» or «MOM» jeans cut into shorts, and an old beat-up cap just because you're on vacation. And your travel squad can't be seen wearing gym clothes and house slippers! God forbid anyone in your travel party shows up at the airport in pajamas -- even if the flight is red-eye. Oversee this process to ensure that your looks **compliment each other and that you two dazzle and spin heads together! Glam. Glam. Glam.**

5 **Hit the gym religiously before your vacation.** Sure, you should be eating right and exercising anyway, but if you're not – OK – get your hips in the gym regularly for three months before your vacation. It's all about the pics. Cake on the lips sits forever on your hips! Repeat it! LOL! After the trip is over, Heck, resume your regular habits – but do what you have to do for the pics!!! **This is crucial.**

6 **Be a true friend and inspect your girls' luggage before traveling.** I know it's hard not to want the spotlight for yourself, but if you're on a girls' trip, all girls should look like they are of the same «squad.» It's awful looking at pictures of girls' trips, and there's that one friend in the pic that appears to have not read the glam memorandum.

7 **All About the Pics.** Whether it's your spouse, your best friend, or whomever, let them know upfront that 90% of **THEIR** vacation will be spent taking pictures of **you. This is a basic human need and a fundamental requirement that must be clarified when the vacation plans are discussed.**

Disclaimer: These are not actual rules and are for entertainment purposes only.

My Fashionista's Travel Vision Board

List the countries that you wish to travel to. The more exotic and fabulous, the better! Go big or stay home!

_____

_____

_____

_____

_____

_____

_____

_____

_____

_____

_____

_____

_____

_____

_____

_____

_____

_____

My Fashionista's Hotel & Resort Vision Board

List the hotels, resorts, villas, and bungalows you wish to stay in during your travels. Be as extravagant as your heart desires!

My Fashionista's Travel Squad Vision Board

List all the names of the people you'd take with you on your travels. Be as free as you please with this list! Your travel squad may include a significant other, a secret admirer, your best friend, or even a hot celebrity!

_____

_____

_____

_____

_____

_____

_____

_____

_____

_____

_____

_____

_____

_____

_____

My Fashionista's Exotic Cuisine Vision Board

List the exotic meals, wines, champagnes, deserts, restaurants, and chefs you wish to experience when traveling. Be as bold and exotic as you want. If you're going to eat a chocolate-smothered fly, who cares? You only live once. LIVE.

_____

_____

_____

_____

_____

_____

_____

_____

_____

_____

_____

_____

_____

_____

_____

_____

Fashionista's Travel Reflections

Travel Date:	**I Felt:**
Vacation Destination:	☐ energetic
Hotel/Resort/Villa:	☐ relaxed
My plans included:	☐ rested
	☐ adventurous
	☐ anxious
	☐ sexy
	☐ tired
I ate the best meal at:	☐ like a party animal
	☐ neutral
	☐ ready to return home
I felt: in my swimwear.	

I felt most adventurous when:

I felt most relaxed when:

I felt most free when:

I felt most connected to my travel companions/family when:

I winded down at the end of the day by:

I was wearing this in my favorite picture:

I didn't have a good time when:

I'm looking forward to planning my next fashionista vacation to:

Fashionista's Travel Reflections

Travel Date:	**I Felt:**
Vacation Destination:	☐ energetic
Hotel/Resort/Villa:	☐ relaxed
My plans included:	☐ rested
	☐ adventurous
	☐ anxious
	☐ sexy
	☐ tired
I ate the best meal at:	☐ like a party animal
	☐ neutral
	☐ ready to return home
I felt: in my swimwear.	

I felt most adventurous when:
I felt most relaxed when:
I felt most free when:
I felt most connected to my travel companions/family when:
I winded down at the end of the day by:
I was wearing this in my favorite picture:
I didn't have a good time when:
I'm looking forward to planning my next fashionista vacation to:

Fashionista's Travel Reflections

Travel Date:	**I Felt:**
Vacation Destination:	☐ energetic
Hotel/Resort/Villa:	☐ relaxed
My plans included:	☐ rested
	☐ adventurous
	☐ anxious
	☐ sexy
	☐ tired
I ate the best meal at:	☐ like a party animal
	☐ neutral
	☐ ready to return home
I felt: in my swimwear.	

I felt most adventurous when:
I felt most relaxed when:
I felt most free when:
I felt most connected to my travel companions/family when:
I winded down at the end of the day by:
I was wearing this in my favorite picture:
I didn't have a good time when:
I'm looking forward to planning my next fashionista vacation to:

Fashionista's Travel Reflections

Travel Date:		**I Felt:**
Vacation Destination:		☐ energetic
Hotel/Resort/Villa:		☐ relaxed
My plans included:		☐ rested
		☐ adventurous
		☐ anxious
		☐ sexy
		☐ tired
I ate the best meal at:		☐ like a party animal
		☐ neutral
		☐ ready to return home
I felt:	in my swimwear.	

I felt most adventurous when:
I felt most relaxed when:
I felt most free when:
I felt most connected to my travel companions/family when:
I winded down at the end of the day by:
I was wearing this in my favorite picture:
I didn't have a good time when:
I'm looking forward to planning my next fashionista vacation to:

Fashionista's Travel Reflections

Travel Date:	**I Felt:**
Vacation Destination:	☐ energetic
Hotel/Resort/Villa:	☐ relaxed
My plans included:	☐ rested
	☐ adventurous
	☐ anxious
	☐ sexy
	☐ tired
I ate the best meal at:	☐ like a party animal
	☐ neutral
	☐ ready to return home
I felt: in my swimwear.	

I felt most adventurous when:

I felt most relaxed when:

I felt most free when:

I felt most connected to my travel companions/family when:

I winded down at the end of the day by:

I was wearing this in my favorite picture:

I didn't have a good time when:

I'm looking forward to planning my next fashionista vacation to:

Fashionista's Travel Reflections

Travel Date:	**I Felt:**
Vacation Destination:	☐ energetic
Hotel/Resort/Villa:	☐ relaxed
My plans included:	☐ rested
	☐ adventurous
	☐ anxious
	☐ sexy
	☐ tired
I ate the best meal at:	☐ like a party animal
	☐ neutral
	☐ ready to return home
I felt: in my swimwear.	

I felt most adventurous when:
I felt most relaxed when:
I felt most free when:
I felt most connected to my travel companions/family when:
I winded down at the end of the day by:
I was wearing this in my favorite picture:
I didn't have a good time when:
I'm looking forward to planning my next fashionista vacation to:

Fashionista's Travel Reflections

Travel Date:	**I Felt:**
Vacation Destination:	☐ energetic
Hotel/Resort/Villa:	☐ relaxed
My plans included:	☐ rested
	☐ adventurous
	☐ anxious
	☐ sexy
	☐ tired
I ate the best meal at:	☐ like a party animal
	☐ neutral
	☐ ready to return home
I felt: _____ in my swimwear.	

I felt most adventurous when:

I felt most relaxed when:

I felt most free when:

I felt most connected to my travel companions/family when:

I winded down at the end of the day by:

I was wearing this in my favorite picture:

I didn't have a good time when:

I'm looking forward to planning my next fashionista vacation to:

Fashionista's Travel Reflections

Travel Date:	**I Felt:**
Vacation Destination:	☐ energetic
Hotel/Resort/Villa:	☐ relaxed
My plans included:	☐ rested
	☐ adventurous
	☐ anxious
	☐ sexy
	☐ tired
I ate the best meal at:	☐ like a party animal
	☐ neutral
I felt: in my swimwear.	☐ ready to return home

I felt most adventurous when:
I felt most relaxed when:
I felt most free when:
I felt most connected to my travel companions/family when:
I winded down at the end of the day by:
I was wearing this in my favorite picture:
I didn't have a good time when:
I'm looking forward to planning my next fashionista vacation to:

Fashionista's Travel Reflections

Travel Date:	**I Felt:**
Vacation Destination:	☐ energetic
Hotel/Resort/Villa:	☐ relaxed
My plans included:	☐ rested
	☐ adventurous
	☐ anxious
	☐ sexy
	☐ tired
I ate the best meal at:	☐ like a party animal
	☐ neutral
	☐ ready to return home
I felt: in my swimwear.	

I felt most adventurous when:
I felt most relaxed when:
I felt most free when:
I felt most connected to my travel companions/family when:
I winded down at the end of the day by:
I was wearing this in my favorite picture:
I didn't have a good time when:
I'm looking forward to planning my next fashionista vacation to:

Fashionista's Travel Reflections

Travel Date:	**I Felt:**
Vacation Destination:	☐ energetic
Hotel/Resort/Villa:	☐ relaxed
My plans included:	☐ rested
	☐ adventurous
	☐ anxious
	☐ sexy
	☐ tired
I ate the best meal at:	☐ like a party animal
	☐ neutral
	☐ ready to return home
I felt: in my swimwear.	

I felt most adventurous when:
I felt most relaxed when:
I felt most free when:
I felt most connected to my travel companions/family when:
I winded down at the end of the day by:
I was wearing this in my favorite picture:
I didn't have a good time when:
I'm looking forward to planning my next fashionista vacation to:

Fashionista's Travel Reflections

Travel Date:	**I Felt:**
Vacation Destination:	☐ energetic
Hotel/Resort/Villa:	☐ relaxed
My plans included:	☐ rested
	☐ adventurous
	☐ anxious
	☐ sexy
	☐ tired
I ate the best meal at:	☐ like a party animal
	☐ neutral
	☐ ready to return home
I felt: in my swimwear.	

I felt most adventurous when:
I felt most relaxed when:
I felt most free when:
I felt most connected to my travel companions/family when:
I winded down at the end of the day by:
I was wearing this in my favorite picture:
I didn't have a good time when:
I'm looking forward to planning my next fashionista vacation to:

Fashionista's Travel Reflections

Travel Date:	**I Felt:**
Vacation Destination:	☐ energetic
Hotel/Resort/Villa:	☐ relaxed
My plans included:	☐ rested
	☐ adventurous
	☐ anxious
	☐ sexy
	☐ tired
I ate the best meal at:	☐ like a party animal
	☐ neutral
I felt: in my swimwear.	☐ ready to return home

I felt most adventurous when:
I felt most relaxed when:
I felt most free when:
I felt most connected to my travel companions/family when:
I winded down at the end of the day by:
I was wearing this in my favorite picture:
I didn't have a good time when:
I'm looking forward to planning my next fashionista vacation to:

Fashionista's Travel Reflections

Travel Date:	**I Felt:**
Vacation Destination:	☐ energetic
Hotel/Resort/Villa:	☐ relaxed
My plans included:	☐ rested
	☐ adventurous
	☐ anxious
	☐ sexy
	☐ tired
I ate the best meal at:	☐ like a party animal
	☐ neutral
	☐ ready to return home
I felt: in my swimwear.	

I felt most adventurous when:

I felt most relaxed when:

I felt most free when:

I felt most connected to my travel companions/family when:

I winded down at the end of the day by:

I was wearing this in my favorite picture:

I didn't have a good time when:

I'm looking forward to planning my next fashionista vacation to:

Fashionista's Travel Reflections

Travel Date:	**I Felt:**
Vacation Destination:	☐ energetic
Hotel/Resort/Villa:	☐ relaxed
My plans included:	☐ rested
	☐ adventurous
	☐ anxious
	☐ sexy
	☐ tired
I ate the best meal at:	☐ like a party animal
	☐ neutral
	☐ ready to return home
I felt: in my swimwear.	

I felt most adventurous when:
I felt most relaxed when:
I felt most free when:
I felt most connected to my travel companions/family when:
I winded down at the end of the day by:
I was wearing this in my favorite picture:
I didn't have a good time when:
I'm looking forward to planning my next fashionista vacation to:

Fashionista's Travel Reflections

Travel Date:	**I Felt:**
Vacation Destination:	☐ energetic
Hotel/Resort/Villa:	☐ relaxed
My plans included:	☐ rested
	☐ adventurous
	☐ anxious
	☐ sexy
	☐ tired
I ate the best meal at:	☐ like a party animal
	☐ neutral
	☐ ready to return home
I felt: in my swimwear.	

I felt most adventurous when:

I felt most relaxed when:

I felt most free when:

I felt most connected to my travel companions/family when:

I winded down at the end of the day by:

I was wearing this in my favorite picture:

I didn't have a good time when:

I'm looking forward to planning my next fashionista vacation to:

Travel Date:	**I Felt:**
Vacation Destination:	☐ energetic
Hotel/Resort/Villa:	☐ relaxed
My plans included:	☐ rested
	☐ adventurous
	☐ anxious
	☐ sexy
	☐ tired
I ate the best meal at:	☐ like a party animal
	☐ neutral
	☐ ready to return home
I felt: in my swimwear.	

I felt most adventurous when:

I felt most relaxed when:

I felt most free when:

I felt most connected to my travel companions/family when:

I winded down at the end of the day by:

I was wearing this in my favorite picture:

I didn't have a good time when:

I'm looking forward to planning my next fashionista vacation to:

Fashionista's Travel Reflections

Travel Date:	**I Felt:**
Vacation Destination:	☐ energetic
Hotel/Resort/Villa:	☐ relaxed
My plans included:	☐ rested
	☐ adventurous
	☐ anxious
	☐ sexy
	☐ tired
I ate the best meal at:	☐ like a party animal
	☐ neutral
	☐ ready to return home
I felt: in my swimwear.	

I felt most adventurous when:
I felt most relaxed when:
I felt most free when:
I felt most connected to my travel companions/family when:
I winded down at the end of the day by:
I was wearing this in my favorite picture:
I didn't have a good time when:
I'm looking forward to planning my next fashionista vacation to:

Fashionista's Travel Reflections

Travel Date:	**I Felt:**
Vacation Destination:	☐ energetic
Hotel/Resort/Villa:	☐ relaxed
My plans included:	☐ rested
	☐ adventurous
	☐ anxious
	☐ sexy
	☐ tired
I ate the best meal at:	☐ like a party animal
	☐ neutral
	☐ ready to return home
I felt: in my swimwear.	

I felt most adventurous when:
I felt most relaxed when:
I felt most free when:
I felt most connected to my travel companions/family when:
I winded down at the end of the day by:
I was wearing this in my favorite picture:
I didn't have a good time when:
I'm looking forward to planning my next fashionista vacation to:

Fashionista's Travel Reflections

Travel Date:	**I Felt:**
Vacation Destination:	☐ energetic
Hotel/Resort/Villa:	☐ relaxed
My plans included:	☐ rested
	☐ adventurous
	☐ anxious
	☐ sexy
	☐ tired
I ate the best meal at:	☐ like a party animal
	☐ neutral
	☐ ready to return home
I felt: in my swimwear.	

I felt most adventurous when:
I felt most relaxed when:
I felt most free when:
I felt most connected to my travel companions/family when:
I winded down at the end of the day by:
I was wearing this in my favorite picture:
I didn't have a good time when:
I'm looking forward to planning my next fashionista vacation to:

Fashionista's Travel Reflections

Travel Date:		**I Felt:**
Vacation Destination:		☐ energetic
Hotel/Resort/Villa:		☐ relaxed
My plans included:		☐ rested
		☐ adventurous
		☐ anxious
		☐ sexy
		☐ tired
I ate the best meal at:		☐ like a party animal
		☐ neutral
		☐ ready to return home
I felt:	in my swimwear.	

I felt most adventurous when:

I felt most relaxed when:

I felt most free when:

I felt most connected to my travel companions/family when:

I winded down at the end of the day by:

I was wearing this in my favorite picture:

I didn't have a good time when:

I'm looking forward to planning my next fashionista vacation to:

Fashionista's Travel Reflections

Travel Date:	**I Felt:**
Vacation Destination:	☐ energetic
Hotel/Resort/Villa:	☐ relaxed
My plans included:	☐ rested
	☐ adventurous
	☐ anxious
	☐ sexy
	☐ tired
I ate the best meal at:	☐ like a party animal
	☐ neutral
	☐ ready to return home
I felt: in my swimwear.	

I felt most adventurous when:

I felt most relaxed when:

I felt most free when:

I felt most connected to my travel companions/family when:

I winded down at the end of the day by:

I was wearing this in my favorite picture:

I didn't have a good time when:

I'm looking forward to planning my next fashionista vacation to:

Fashionista's Travel Reflections

Travel Date:	**I Felt:**
Vacation Destination:	☐ energetic
Hotel/Resort/Villa:	☐ relaxed
My plans included:	☐ rested
	☐ adventurous
	☐ anxious
	☐ sexy
	☐ tired
I ate the best meal at:	☐ like a party animal
	☐ neutral
	☐ ready to return home
I felt: _____ in my swimwear.	

I felt most adventurous when:
I felt most relaxed when:
I felt most free when:
I felt most connected to my travel companions/family when:
I winded down at the end of the day by:
I was wearing this in my favorite picture:
I didn't have a good time when:
I'm looking forward to planning my next fashionista vacation to:

Fashionista's Travel Reflections

Travel Date:	**I Felt:**
Vacation Destination:	☐ energetic
Hotel/Resort/Villa:	☐ relaxed
My plans included:	☐ rested
	☐ adventurous
	☐ anxious
	☐ sexy
	☐ tired
I ate the best meal at:	☐ like a party animal
	☐ neutral
	☐ ready to return home
I felt: in my swimwear.	

I felt most adventurous when:
I felt most relaxed when:
I felt most free when:
I felt most connected to my travel companions/family when:
I winded down at the end of the day by:
I was wearing this in my favorite picture:
I didn't have a good time when:
I'm looking forward to planning my next fashionista vacation to:

Fashionista's Travel Reflections

Travel Date:	I Felt:
Vacation Destination:	☐ energetic
Hotel/Resort/Villa:	☐ relaxed
My plans included:	☐ rested
	☐ adventurous
	☐ anxious
	☐ sexy
	☐ tired
I ate the best meal at:	☐ like a party animal
	☐ neutral
	☐ ready to return home
I felt: in my swimwear.	

I felt most adventurous when:

I felt most relaxed when:

I felt most free when:

I felt most connected to my travel companions/family when:

I winded down at the end of the day by:

I was wearing this in my favorite picture:

I didn't have a good time when:

I'm looking forward to planning my next fashionista vacation to:

Fashionista's Travel Reflections

Travel Date:	**I Felt:**
Vacation Destination:	☐ energetic
Hotel/Resort/Villa:	☐ relaxed
My plans included:	☐ rested
	☐ adventurous
	☐ anxious
	☐ sexy
	☐ tired
I ate the best meal at:	☐ like a party animal
	☐ neutral
	☐ ready to return home
I felt: in my swimwear.	

I felt most adventurous when:

I felt most relaxed when:

I felt most free when:

I felt most connected to my travel companions/family when:

I winded down at the end of the day by:

I was wearing this in my favorite picture:

I didn't have a good time when:

I'm looking forward to planning my next fashionista vacation to:

Fashionista's Travel Reflections

Travel Date:	**I Felt:**
Vacation Destination:	☐ energetic
Hotel/Resort/Villa:	☐ relaxed
My plans included:	☐ rested
	☐ adventurous
	☐ anxious
	☐ sexy
	☐ tired
I ate the best meal at:	☐ like a party animal
	☐ neutral
	☐ ready to return home
I felt: in my swimwear.	

I felt most adventurous when:

I felt most relaxed when:

I felt most free when:

I felt most connected to my travel companions/family when:

I winded down at the end of the day by:

I was wearing this in my favorite picture:

I didn't have a good time when:

I'm looking forward to planning my next fashionista vacation to:

Fashionista's Travel Reflections

Travel Date:	**I Felt:**
Vacation Destination:	☐ energetic
Hotel/Resort/Villa:	☐ relaxed
My plans included:	☐ rested
	☐ adventurous
	☐ anxious
	☐ sexy
	☐ tired
I ate the best meal at:	☐ like a party animal
	☐ neutral
	☐ ready to return home
I felt: in my swimwear.	

I felt most adventurous when:

I felt most relaxed when:

I felt most free when:

I felt most connected to my travel companions/family when:

I winded down at the end of the day by:

I was wearing this in my favorite picture:

I didn't have a good time when:

I'm looking forward to planning my next fashionista vacation to:

Fashionista's Travel Reflections

Travel Date:	**I Felt:**
Vacation Destination:	☐ energetic
Hotel/Resort/Villa:	☐ relaxed
My plans included:	☐ rested
	☐ adventurous
	☐ anxious
	☐ sexy
	☐ tired
I ate the best meal at:	☐ like a party animal
	☐ neutral
I felt: in my swimwear.	☐ ready to return home

I felt most adventurous when:

I felt most relaxed when:

I felt most free when:

I felt most connected to my travel companions/family when:

I winded down at the end of the day by:

I was wearing this in my favorite picture:

I didn't have a good time when:

I'm looking forward to planning my next fashionista vacation to:

Fashionista's Travel Reflections

Travel Date:	**I Felt:**
Vacation Destination:	☐ energetic
Hotel/Resort/Villa:	☐ relaxed
My plans included:	☐ rested
	☐ adventurous
	☐ anxious
	☐ sexy
	☐ tired
I ate the best meal at:	☐ like a party animal
	☐ neutral
	☐ ready to return home
I felt: in my swimwear.	

I felt most adventurous when:

I felt most relaxed when:

I felt most free when:

I felt most connected to my travel companions/family when:

I winded down at the end of the day by:

I was wearing this in my favorite picture:

I didn't have a good time when:

I'm looking forward to planning my next fashionista vacation to:

Fashionista's Travel Reflections

Travel Date:	**I Felt:**
Vacation Destination:	☐ energetic
Hotel/Resort/Villa:	☐ relaxed
My plans included:	☐ rested
	☐ adventurous
	☐ anxious
	☐ sexy
	☐ tired
I ate the best meal at:	☐ like a party animal
	☐ neutral
	☐ ready to return home
I felt: in my swimwear.	

I felt most adventurous when:
I felt most relaxed when:
I felt most free when:
I felt most connected to my travel companions/family when:
I winded down at the end of the day by:
I was wearing this in my favorite picture:
I didn't have a good time when:
I'm looking forward to planning my next fashionista vacation to:

Fashionista's Travel Reflections

Travel Date:	**I Felt:**
Vacation Destination:	☐ energetic
Hotel/Resort/Villa:	☐ relaxed
My plans included:	☐ rested
	☐ adventurous
	☐ anxious
	☐ sexy
	☐ tired
I ate the best meal at:	☐ like a party animal
	☐ neutral
	☐ ready to return home
I felt: in my swimwear.	

I felt most adventurous when:
I felt most relaxed when:
I felt most free when:
I felt most connected to my travel companions/family when:
I winded down at the end of the day by:
I was wearing this in my favorite picture:
I didn't have a good time when:
I'm looking forward to planning my next fashionista vacation to:

Fashionista's Travel Reflections

Travel Date:	**I Felt:**
Vacation Destination:	☐ energetic
Hotel/Resort/Villa:	☐ relaxed
My plans included:	☐ rested
	☐ adventurous
	☐ anxious
	☐ sexy
	☐ tired
I ate the best meal at:	☐ like a party animal
	☐ neutral
	☐ ready to return home
I felt: in my swimwear.	

I felt most adventurous when:
I felt most relaxed when:
I felt most free when:
I felt most connected to my travel companions/family when:
I winded down at the end of the day by:
I was wearing this in my favorite picture:
I didn't have a good time when:
I'm looking forward to planning my next fashionista vacation to:

Fashionista's Travel Reflections

Travel Date:	**I Felt:**
Vacation Destination:	☐ energetic
Hotel/Resort/Villa:	☐ relaxed
My plans included:	☐ rested
	☐ adventurous
	☐ anxious
	☐ sexy
	☐ tired
I ate the best meal at:	☐ like a party animal
	☐ neutral
	☐ ready to return home
I felt: in my swimwear.	

I felt most adventurous when:

I felt most relaxed when:

I felt most free when:

I felt most connected to my travel companions/family when:

I winded down at the end of the day by:

I was wearing this in my favorite picture:

I didn't have a good time when:

I'm looking forward to planning my next fashionista vacation to:

Fashionista's Travel Reflections

Travel Date:		**I Felt:**
Vacation Destination:		☐ energetic
Hotel/Resort/Villa:		☐ relaxed
My plans included:		☐ rested
		☐ adventurous
		☐ anxious
		☐ sexy
		☐ tired
I ate the best meal at:		☐ like a party animal
		☐ neutral
		☐ ready to return home
I felt:	in my swimwear.	

I felt most adventurous when:

I felt most relaxed when:

I felt most free when:

I felt most connected to my travel companions/family when:

I winded down at the end of the day by:

I was wearing this in my favorite picture:

I didn't have a good time when:

I'm looking forward to planning my next fashionista vacation to:

Fashionista's Travel Reflections

Travel Date:	**I Felt:**
Vacation Destination:	☐ energetic
Hotel/Resort/Villa:	☐ relaxed
My plans included:	☐ rested
	☐ adventurous
	☐ anxious
	☐ sexy
	☐ tired
I ate the best meal at:	☐ like a party animal
	☐ neutral
	☐ ready to return home
I felt: in my swimwear.	

I felt most adventurous when:
I felt most relaxed when:
I felt most free when:
I felt most connected to my travel companions/family when:
I winded down at the end of the day by:
I was wearing this in my favorite picture:
I didn't have a good time when:
I'm looking forward to planning my next fashionista vacation to:

Fashionista's Travel Reflections

Travel Date:	**I Felt:**
Vacation Destination:	☐ energetic
Hotel/Resort/Villa:	☐ relaxed
My plans included:	☐ rested
	☐ adventurous
	☐ anxious
	☐ sexy
	☐ tired
I ate the best meal at:	☐ like a party animal
	☐ neutral
	☐ ready to return home
I felt: in my swimwear.	

I felt most adventurous when:
I felt most relaxed when:
I felt most free when:
I felt most connected to my travel companions/family when:
I winded down at the end of the day by:
I was wearing this in my favorite picture:
I didn't have a good time when:
I'm looking forward to planning my next fashionista vacation to:

Fashionista's Travel Reflections

Travel Date:	**I Felt:**
Vacation Destination:	☐ energetic
Hotel/Resort/Villa:	☐ relaxed
My plans included:	☐ rested
	☐ adventurous
	☐ anxious
	☐ sexy
	☐ tired
I ate the best meal at:	☐ like a party animal
	☐ neutral
	☐ ready to return home
I felt: in my swimwear.	

I felt most adventurous when:

I felt most relaxed when:

I felt most free when:

I felt most connected to my travel companions/family when:

I winded down at the end of the day by:

I was wearing this in my favorite picture:

I didn't have a good time when:

I'm looking forward to planning my next fashionista vacation to:

Fashionista's Travel Reflections

Travel Date:	**I Felt:**
Vacation Destination:	☐ energetic
Hotel/Resort/Villa:	☐ relaxed
My plans included:	☐ rested
	☐ adventurous
	☐ anxious
	☐ sexy
	☐ tired
I ate the best meal at:	☐ like a party animal
	☐ neutral
	☐ ready to return home
I felt: _____ in my swimwear.	

I felt most adventurous when:

I felt most relaxed when:

I felt most free when:

I felt most connected to my travel companions/family when:

I winded down at the end of the day by:

I was wearing this in my favorite picture:

I didn't have a good time when:

I'm looking forward to planning my next fashionista vacation to:

Fashionista's Travel Reflections

Travel Date:	**I Felt:**
Vacation Destination:	☐ energetic
Hotel/Resort/Villa:	☐ relaxed
My plans included:	☐ rested
	☐ adventurous
	☐ anxious
	☐ sexy
	☐ tired
I ate the best meal at:	☐ like a party animal
	☐ neutral
	☐ ready to return home
I felt: in my swimwear.	

I felt most adventurous when:

I felt most relaxed when:

I felt most free when:

I felt most connected to my travel companions/family when:

I winded down at the end of the day by:

I was wearing this in my favorite picture:

I didn't have a good time when:

I'm looking forward to planning my next fashionista vacation to:

Fashionista's Travel Reflections

Travel Date:	**I Felt:**
Vacation Destination:	☐ energetic
Hotel/Resort/Villa:	☐ relaxed
My plans included:	☐ rested
	☐ adventurous
	☐ anxious
	☐ sexy
	☐ tired
I ate the best meal at:	☐ like a party animal
	☐ neutral
	☐ ready to return home
I felt: in my swimwear.	

I felt most adventurous when:

I felt most relaxed when:

I felt most free when:

I felt most connected to my travel companions/family when:

I winded down at the end of the day by:

I was wearing this in my favorite picture:

I didn't have a good time when:

I'm looking forward to planning my next fashionista vacation to:

Fashionista's Travel Reflections

Travel Date:		I Felt:
Vacation Destination:		☐ energetic
Hotel/Resort/Villa:		☐ relaxed
My plans included:		☐ rested
		☐ adventurous
		☐ anxious
		☐ sexy
		☐ tired
I ate the best meal at:		☐ like a party animal
		☐ neutral
		☐ ready to return home
I felt:	in my swimwear.	

I felt most adventurous when:
I felt most relaxed when:
I felt most free when:
I felt most connected to my travel companions/family when:
I winded down at the end of the day by:
I was wearing this in my favorite picture:
I didn't have a good time when:
I'm looking forward to planning my next fashionista vacation to:

Fashionista's Travel Reflections

Travel Date:	**I Felt:**
Vacation Destination:	☐ energetic
Hotel/Resort/Villa:	☐ relaxed
My plans included:	☐ rested
	☐ adventurous
	☐ anxious
	☐ sexy
	☐ tired
I ate the best meal at:	☐ like a party animal
	☐ neutral
	☐ ready to return home
I felt: in my swimwear.	

I felt most adventurous when:
I felt most relaxed when:
I felt most free when:
I felt most connected to my travel companions/family when:
I winded down at the end of the day by:
I was wearing this in my favorite picture:
I didn't have a good time when:
I'm looking forward to planning my next fashionista vacation to:

Fashionista's Travel Reflections

Travel Date:	**I Felt:**
Vacation Destination:	☐ energetic
Hotel/Resort/Villa:	☐ relaxed
My plans included:	☐ rested
	☐ adventurous
	☐ anxious
	☐ sexy
	☐ tired
I ate the best meal at:	☐ like a party animal
	☐ neutral
	☐ ready to return home
I felt: in my swimwear.	

I felt most adventurous when:

I felt most relaxed when:

I felt most free when:

I felt most connected to my travel companions/family when:

I winded down at the end of the day by:

I was wearing this in my favorite picture:

I didn't have a good time when:

I'm looking forward to planning my next fashionista vacation to:

Fashionista's Travel Reflections

Travel Date:	**I Felt:**
Vacation Destination:	☐ energetic
Hotel/Resort/Villa:	☐ relaxed
My plans included:	☐ rested
	☐ adventurous
	☐ anxious
	☐ sexy
	☐ tired
I ate the best meal at:	☐ like a party animal
	☐ neutral
	☐ ready to return home
I felt: _____ in my swimwear.	

I felt most adventurous when:

I felt most relaxed when:

I felt most free when:

I felt most connected to my travel companions/family when:

I winded down at the end of the day by:

I was wearing this in my favorite picture:

I didn't have a good time when:

I'm looking forward to planning my next fashionista vacation to:

Fashionista's Travel Reflections

Travel Date:	**I Felt:**
Vacation Destination:	☐ energetic
Hotel/Resort/Villa:	☐ relaxed
My plans included:	☐ rested
	☐ adventurous
	☐ anxious
	☐ sexy
	☐ tired
I ate the best meal at:	☐ like a party animal
	☐ neutral
	☐ ready to return home
I felt: in my swimwear.	

I felt most adventurous when:

I felt most relaxed when:

I felt most free when:

I felt most connected to my travel companions/family when:

I winded down at the end of the day by:

I was wearing this in my favorite picture:

I didn't have a good time when:

I'm looking forward to planning my next fashionista vacation to:

Fashionista's Travel Reflections

Travel Date:	**I Felt:**
Vacation Destination:	☐ energetic
Hotel/Resort/Villa:	☐ relaxed
My plans included:	☐ rested
	☐ adventurous
	☐ anxious
	☐ sexy
	☐ tired
I ate the best meal at:	☐ like a party animal
	☐ neutral
	☐ ready to return home
I felt: in my swimwear.	

I felt most adventurous when:
I felt most relaxed when:
I felt most free when:
I felt most connected to my travel companions/family when:
I winded down at the end of the day by:
I was wearing this in my favorite picture:
I didn't have a good time when:
I'm looking forward to planning my next fashionista vacation to:

Fashionista's Travel Reflections

Travel Date:	**I Felt:**
Vacation Destination:	☐ energetic
Hotel/Resort/Villa:	☐ relaxed
My plans included:	☐ rested
	☐ adventurous
	☐ anxious
	☐ sexy
	☐ tired
I ate the best meal at:	☐ like a party animal
	☐ neutral
	☐ ready to return home
I felt: in my swimwear.	

I felt most adventurous when:
I felt most relaxed when:
I felt most free when:
I felt most connected to my travel companions/family when:
I winded down at the end of the day by:
I was wearing this in my favorite picture:
I didn't have a good time when:
I'm looking forward to planning my next fashionista vacation to:

Fashionista's Travel Reflections

Travel Date:	**I Felt:**
Vacation Destination:	☐ energetic
Hotel/Resort/Villa:	☐ relaxed
My plans included:	☐ rested
	☐ adventurous
	☐ anxious
	☐ sexy
	☐ tired
I ate the best meal at:	☐ like a party animal
	☐ neutral
	☐ ready to return home
I felt: in my swimwear.	

I felt most adventurous when:
I felt most relaxed when:
I felt most free when:
I felt most connected to my travel companions/family when:
I winded down at the end of the day by:
I was wearing this in my favorite picture:
I didn't have a good time when:
I'm looking forward to planning my next fashionista vacation to:

Fashionista's Travel Reflections

Travel Date:	**I Felt:**
Vacation Destination:	☐ energetic
Hotel/Resort/Villa:	☐ relaxed
My plans included:	☐ rested
	☐ adventurous
	☐ anxious
	☐ sexy
	☐ tired
I ate the best meal at:	☐ like a party animal
	☐ neutral
I felt: in my swimwear.	☐ ready to return home

I felt most adventurous when:

I felt most relaxed when:

I felt most free when:

I felt most connected to my travel companions/family when:

I winded down at the end of the day by:

I was wearing this in my favorite picture:

I didn't have a good time when:

I'm looking forward to planning my next fashionista vacation to:

Fashionista's Travel Reflections

Travel Date:	**I Felt:**
Vacation Destination:	☐ energetic
Hotel/Resort/Villa:	☐ relaxed
My plans included:	☐ rested
	☐ adventurous
	☐ anxious
	☐ sexy
	☐ tired
I ate the best meal at:	☐ like a party animal
	☐ neutral
	☐ ready to return home
I felt: in my swimwear.	

I felt most adventurous when:
I felt most relaxed when:
I felt most free when:
I felt most connected to my travel companions/family when:
I winded down at the end of the day by:
I was wearing this in my favorite picture:
I didn't have a good time when:
I'm looking forward to planning my next fashionista vacation to:

Fashionista's Travel Reflections

Travel Date:	**I Felt:**
Vacation Destination:	☐ energetic
Hotel/Resort/Villa:	☐ relaxed
My plans included:	☐ rested
	☐ adventurous
	☐ anxious
	☐ sexy
	☐ tired
I ate the best meal at:	☐ like a party animal
	☐ neutral
	☐ ready to return home
I felt: in my swimwear.	

I felt most adventurous when:
I felt most relaxed when:
I felt most free when:
I felt most connected to my travel companions/family when:
I winded down at the end of the day by:
I was wearing this in my favorite picture:
I didn't have a good time when:
I'm looking forward to planning my next fashionista vacation to:

Travel Date:	**I Felt:**
Vacation Destination:	☐ energetic
Hotel/Resort/Villa:	☐ relaxed
My plans included:	☐ rested
	☐ adventurous
	☐ anxious
	☐ sexy
	☐ tired
I ate the best meal at:	☐ like a party animal
	☐ neutral
	☐ ready to return home
I felt: in my swimwear.	

I felt most adventurous when:
I felt most relaxed when:
I felt most free when:
I felt most connected to my travel companions/family when:
I winded down at the end of the day by:
I was wearing this in my favorite picture:
I didn't have a good time when:
I'm looking forward to planning my next fashionista vacation to:

Fashionista's Travel Reflections

Travel Date:	**I Felt:**
Vacation Destination:	☐ energetic
Hotel/Resort/Villa:	☐ relaxed
My plans included:	☐ rested
	☐ adventurous
	☐ anxious
	☐ sexy
	☐ tired
I ate the best meal at:	☐ like a party animal
	☐ neutral
	☐ ready to return home
I felt: in my swimwear.	

I felt most adventurous when:

I felt most relaxed when:

I felt most free when:

I felt most connected to my travel companions/family when:

I winded down at the end of the day by:

I was wearing this in my favorite picture:

I didn't have a good time when:

I'm looking forward to planning my next fashionista vacation to:

Travel Date:		I Felt:
Vacation Destination:		☐ energetic
Hotel/Resort/Villa:		☐ relaxed
My plans included:		☐ rested
		☐ adventurous
		☐ anxious
		☐ sexy
		☐ tired
I ate the best meal at:		☐ like a party animal
		☐ neutral
		☐ ready to return home
I felt:	in my swimwear.	
I felt most adventurous when:		
I felt most relaxed when:		
I felt most free when:		
I felt most connected to my travel companions/family when:		
I winded down at the end of the day by:		
I was wearing this in my favorite picture:		
I didn't have a good time when:		
I'm looking forward to planning my next fashionista vacation to:		

Fashionista's Travel Reflections

Travel Date:	**I Felt:**
Vacation Destination:	☐ energetic
Hotel/Resort/Villa:	☐ relaxed
My plans included:	☐ rested
	☐ adventurous
	☐ anxious
	☐ sexy
	☐ tired
I ate the best meal at:	☐ like a party animal
	☐ neutral
	☐ ready to return home
I felt: in my swimwear.	

I felt most adventurous when:

I felt most relaxed when:

I felt most free when:

I felt most connected to my travel companions/family when:

I winded down at the end of the day by:

I was wearing this in my favorite picture:

I didn't have a good time when:

I'm looking forward to planning my next fashionista vacation to:

Fashionista's Travel Reflections

Travel Date:	**I Felt:**
Vacation Destination:	☐ energetic
Hotel/Resort/Villa:	☐ relaxed
My plans included:	☐ rested
	☐ adventurous
	☐ anxious
	☐ sexy
	☐ tired
I ate the best meal at:	☐ like a party animal
	☐ neutral
	☐ ready to return home
I felt: in my swimwear.	

I felt most adventurous when:

I felt most relaxed when:

I felt most free when:

I felt most connected to my travel companions/family when:

I winded down at the end of the day by:

I was wearing this in my favorite picture:

I didn't have a good time when:

I'm looking forward to planning my next fashionista vacation to:

Fashionista's Travel Reflections

Travel Date:	**I Felt:**
Vacation Destination:	☐ energetic
Hotel/Resort/Villa:	☐ relaxed
My plans included:	☐ rested
	☐ adventurous
	☐ anxious
	☐ sexy
	☐ tired
I ate the best meal at:	☐ like a party animal
	☐ neutral
	☐ ready to return home
I felt: in my swimwear.	

I felt most adventurous when:

I felt most relaxed when:

I felt most free when:

I felt most connected to my travel companions/family when:

I winded down at the end of the day by:

I was wearing this in my favorite picture:

I didn't have a good time when:

I'm looking forward to planning my next fashionista vacation to:

Fashionista's Travel Reflections

Travel Date:	**I Felt:**
Vacation Destination:	☐ energetic
Hotel/Resort/Villa:	☐ relaxed
My plans included:	☐ rested
	☐ adventurous
	☐ anxious
	☐ sexy
	☐ tired
I ate the best meal at:	☐ like a party animal
	☐ neutral
	☐ ready to return home
I felt: in my swimwear.	

I felt most adventurous when:
I felt most relaxed when:
I felt most free when:
I felt most connected to my travel companions/family when:
I winded down at the end of the day by:
I was wearing this in my favorite picture:
I didn't have a good time when:
I'm looking forward to planning my next fashionista vacation to:

Fashionista's Travel Reflections

Travel Date:	**I Felt:**
Vacation Destination:	☐ energetic
Hotel/Resort/Villa:	☐ relaxed
My plans included:	☐ rested
	☐ adventurous
	☐ anxious
	☐ sexy
	☐ tired
I ate the best meal at:	☐ like a party animal
	☐ neutral
	☐ ready to return home
I felt: in my swimwear.	

I felt most adventurous when:

I felt most relaxed when:

I felt most free when:

I felt most connected to my travel companions/family when:

I winded down at the end of the day by:

I was wearing this in my favorite picture:

I didn't have a good time when:

I'm looking forward to planning my next fashionista vacation to:

Fashionista's Travel Reflections

Travel Date:	
Vacation Destination:	**I Felt:**
Hotel/Resort/Villa:	☐ energetic
My plans included:	☐ relaxed
	☐ rested
	☐ adventurous
	☐ anxious
	☐ sexy
	☐ tired
I ate the best meal at:	☐ like a party animal
	☐ neutral
	☐ ready to return home
I felt: in my swimwear.	

I felt most adventurous when:

I felt most relaxed when:

I felt most free when:

I felt most connected to my travel companions/family when:

I winded down at the end of the day by:

I was wearing this in my favorite picture:

I didn't have a good time when:

I'm looking forward to planning my next fashionista vacation to:

Fashionista's Travel Reflections

Travel Date:	**I Felt:**
Vacation Destination:	☐ energetic
Hotel/Resort/Villa:	☐ relaxed
My plans included:	☐ rested
	☐ adventurous
	☐ anxious
	☐ sexy
	☐ tired
I ate the best meal at:	☐ like a party animal
	☐ neutral
	☐ ready to return home
I felt: in my swimwear.	

I felt most adventurous when:
I felt most relaxed when:
I felt most free when:
I felt most connected to my travel companions/family when:
I winded down at the end of the day by:
I was wearing this in my favorite picture:
I didn't have a good time when:
I'm looking forward to planning my next fashionista vacation to:

Fashionista's Travel Reflections

Travel Date:	**I Felt:**
Vacation Destination:	☐ energetic
Hotel/Resort/Villa:	☐ relaxed
My plans included:	☐ rested
	☐ adventurous
	☐ anxious
	☐ sexy
	☐ tired
I ate the best meal at:	☐ like a party animal
	☐ neutral
	☐ ready to return home
I felt: in my swimwear.	

I felt most adventurous when:
I felt most relaxed when:
I felt most free when:
I felt most connected to my travel companions/family when:
I winded down at the end of the day by:
I was wearing this in my favorite picture:
I didn't have a good time when:
I'm looking forward to planning my next fashionista vacation to:

Fashionista's Travel Reflections

Travel Date:	**I Felt:**
Vacation Destination:	☐ energetic
Hotel/Resort/Villa:	☐ relaxed
My plans included:	☐ rested
	☐ adventurous
	☐ anxious
	☐ sexy
	☐ tired
I ate the best meal at:	☐ like a party animal
	☐ neutral
	☐ ready to return home
I felt: in my swimwear.	

I felt most adventurous when:
I felt most relaxed when:
I felt most free when:
I felt most connected to my travel companions/family when:
I winded down at the end of the day by:
I was wearing this in my favorite picture:
I didn't have a good time when:
I'm looking forward to planning my next fashionista vacation to:

Fashionista's Travel Reflections

Travel Date:	**I Felt:**
Vacation Destination:	☐ energetic
Hotel/Resort/Villa:	☐ relaxed
My plans included:	☐ rested
	☐ adventurous
	☐ anxious
	☐ sexy
	☐ tired
I ate the best meal at:	☐ like a party animal
	☐ neutral
	☐ ready to return home
I felt: in my swimwear.	

I felt most adventurous when:

I felt most relaxed when:

I felt most free when:

I felt most connected to my travel companions/family when:

I winded down at the end of the day by:

I was wearing this in my favorite picture:

I didn't have a good time when:

I'm looking forward to planning my next fashionista vacation to:

Fashionista's Travel Reflections

Travel Date:	**I Felt:**
Vacation Destination:	☐ energetic
Hotel/Resort/Villa:	☐ relaxed
My plans included:	☐ rested
	☐ adventurous
	☐ anxious
	☐ sexy
	☐ tired
I ate the best meal at:	☐ like a party animal
	☐ neutral
	☐ ready to return home
I felt: _____ in my swimwear.	

I felt most adventurous when:

I felt most relaxed when:

I felt most free when:

I felt most connected to my travel companions/family when:

I winded down at the end of the day by:

I was wearing this in my favorite picture:

I didn't have a good time when:

I'm looking forward to planning my next fashionista vacation to:

Fashionista's Travel Reflections

Travel Date:	**I Felt:**
Vacation Destination:	☐ energetic
Hotel/Resort/Villa:	☐ relaxed
My plans included:	☐ rested
	☐ adventurous
	☐ anxious
	☐ sexy
	☐ tired
I ate the best meal at:	☐ like a party animal
	☐ neutral
	☐ ready to return home
I felt: in my swimwear.	

I felt most adventurous when:
I felt most relaxed when:
I felt most free when:
I felt most connected to my travel companions/family when:
I winded down at the end of the day by:
I was wearing this in my favorite picture:
I didn't have a good time when:
I'm looking forward to planning my next fashionista vacation to:

Fashionista's Travel Reflections

Travel Date:	**I Felt:**
Vacation Destination:	☐ energetic
Hotel/Resort/Villa:	☐ relaxed
My plans included:	☐ rested
	☐ adventurous
	☐ anxious
	☐ sexy
	☐ tired
I ate the best meal at:	☐ like a party animal
	☐ neutral
	☐ ready to return home
I felt: in my swimwear.	

I felt most adventurous when:

I felt most relaxed when:

I felt most free when:

I felt most connected to my travel companions/family when:

I winded down at the end of the day by:

I was wearing this in my favorite picture:

I didn't have a good time when:

I'm looking forward to planning my next fashionista vacation to:

Fashionista's Travel Reflections

Travel Date:	**I Felt:**
Vacation Destination:	☐ energetic
Hotel/Resort/Villa:	☐ relaxed
My plans included:	☐ rested
	☐ adventurous
	☐ anxious
	☐ sexy
	☐ tired
I ate the best meal at:	☐ like a party animal
	☐ neutral
I felt: in my swimwear.	☐ ready to return home

I felt most adventurous when:
I felt most relaxed when:
I felt most free when:
I felt most connected to my travel companions/family when:
I winded down at the end of the day by:
I was wearing this in my favorite picture:
I didn't have a good time when:
I'm looking forward to planning my next fashionista vacation to:

Fashionista's Travel Reflections

Travel Date:	**I Felt:**
Vacation Destination:	☐ energetic
Hotel/Resort/Villa:	☐ relaxed
My plans included:	☐ rested
	☐ adventurous
	☐ anxious
	☐ sexy
	☐ tired
I ate the best meal at:	☐ like a party animal
	☐ neutral
	☐ ready to return home
I felt: _____ in my swimwear.	

I felt most adventurous when:

I felt most relaxed when:

I felt most free when:

I felt most connected to my travel companions/family when:

I winded down at the end of the day by:

I was wearing this in my favorite picture:

I didn't have a good time when:

I'm looking forward to planning my next fashionista vacation to:

Fashionista's Travel Reflections

Travel Date:	**I Felt:**
Vacation Destination:	☐ energetic
Hotel/Resort/Villa:	☐ relaxed
My plans included:	☐ rested
	☐ adventurous
	☐ anxious
	☐ sexy
	☐ tired
I ate the best meal at:	☐ like a party animal
	☐ neutral
	☐ ready to return home
I felt: in my swimwear.	

I felt most adventurous when:
I felt most relaxed when:
I felt most free when:
I felt most connected to my travel companions/family when:
I winded down at the end of the day by:
I was wearing this in my favorite picture:
I didn't have a good time when:
I'm looking forward to planning my next fashionista vacation to:

Fashionista's Travel Reflections

Travel Date:	**I Felt:**
Vacation Destination:	☐ energetic
Hotel/Resort/Villa:	☐ relaxed
My plans included:	☐ rested
	☐ adventurous
	☐ anxious
	☐ sexy
	☐ tired
I ate the best meal at:	☐ like a party animal
	☐ neutral
	☐ ready to return home
I felt: in my swimwear.	

I felt most adventurous when:
I felt most relaxed when:
I felt most free when:
I felt most connected to my travel companions/family when:
I winded down at the end of the day by:
I was wearing this in my favorite picture:
I didn't have a good time when:
I'm looking forward to planning my next fashionista vacation to:

Fashionista's Travel Reflections

Travel Date:	**I Felt:**
Vacation Destination:	☐ energetic
Hotel/Resort/Villa:	☐ relaxed
My plans included:	☐ rested
	☐ adventurous
	☐ anxious
	☐ sexy
	☐ tired
I ate the best meal at:	☐ like a party animal
	☐ neutral
	☐ ready to return home
I felt: in my swimwear.	

I felt most adventurous when:
I felt most relaxed when:
I felt most free when:
I felt most connected to my travel companions/family when:
I winded down at the end of the day by:
I was wearing this in my favorite picture:
I didn't have a good time when:
I'm looking forward to planning my next fashionista vacation to:

Fashionista's Travel Reflections

Travel Date:	**I Felt:**
Vacation Destination:	☐ energetic
Hotel/Resort/Villa:	☐ relaxed
My plans included:	☐ rested
	☐ adventurous
	☐ anxious
	☐ sexy
	☐ tired
I ate the best meal at:	☐ like a party animal
	☐ neutral
	☐ ready to return home
I felt: in my swimwear.	

I felt most adventurous when:

I felt most relaxed when:

I felt most free when:

I felt most connected to my travel companions/family when:

I winded down at the end of the day by:

I was wearing this in my favorite picture:

I didn't have a good time when:

I'm looking forward to planning my next fashionista vacation to:

Fashionista's Travel Reflections

Travel Date:	**I Felt:**
Vacation Destination:	☐ energetic
Hotel/Resort/Villa:	☐ relaxed
My plans included:	☐ rested
	☐ adventurous
	☐ anxious
	☐ sexy
	☐ tired
I ate the best meal at:	☐ like a party animal
	☐ neutral
	☐ ready to return home
I felt: in my swimwear.	

I felt most adventurous when:

I felt most relaxed when:

I felt most free when:

I felt most connected to my travel companions/family when:

I winded down at the end of the day by:

I was wearing this in my favorite picture:

I didn't have a good time when:

I'm looking forward to planning my next fashionista vacation to:

Fashionista's Travel Reflections

Travel Date:	**I Felt:**
Vacation Destination:	☐ energetic
Hotel/Resort/Villa:	☐ relaxed
My plans included:	☐ rested
	☐ adventurous
	☐ anxious
	☐ sexy
	☐ tired
I ate the best meal at:	☐ like a party animal
	☐ neutral
	☐ ready to return home
I felt: in my swimwear.	

I felt most adventurous when:
I felt most relaxed when:
I felt most free when:
I felt most connected to my travel companions/family when:
I winded down at the end of the day by:
I was wearing this in my favorite picture:
I didn't have a good time when:
I'm looking forward to planning my next fashionista vacation to:

Fashionista's Travel Reflections

Travel Date:	**I Felt:**
Vacation Destination:	☐ energetic
Hotel/Resort/Villa:	☐ relaxed
My plans included:	☐ rested
	☐ adventurous
	☐ anxious
	☐ sexy
	☐ tired
I ate the best meal at:	☐ like a party animal
	☐ neutral
	☐ ready to return home
I felt: in my swimwear.	

I felt most adventurous when:

I felt most relaxed when:

I felt most free when:

I felt most connected to my travel companions/family when:

I winded down at the end of the day by:

I was wearing this in my favorite picture:

I didn't have a good time when:

I'm looking forward to planning my next fashionista vacation to:

Fashionista's Travel Reflections

Travel Date:	**I Felt:**
Vacation Destination:	☐ energetic
Hotel/Resort/Villa:	☐ relaxed
My plans included:	☐ rested
	☐ adventurous
	☐ anxious
	☐ sexy
	☐ tired
I ate the best meal at:	☐ like a party animal
	☐ neutral
	☐ ready to return home
I felt: in my swimwear.	

I felt most adventurous when:
I felt most relaxed when:
I felt most free when:
I felt most connected to my travel companions/family when:
I winded down at the end of the day by:
I was wearing this in my favorite picture:
I didn't have a good time when:
I'm looking forward to planning my next fashionista vacation to:

Fashionista's Travel Reflections

Travel Date:	**I Felt:**
Vacation Destination:	☐ energetic
Hotel/Resort/Villa:	☐ relaxed
My plans included:	☐ rested
	☐ adventurous
	☐ anxious
	☐ sexy
	☐ tired
I ate the best meal at:	☐ like a party animal
	☐ neutral
	☐ ready to return home
I felt: in my swimwear.	

I felt most adventurous when:

I felt most relaxed when:

I felt most free when:

I felt most connected to my travel companions/family when:

I winded down at the end of the day by:

I was wearing this in my favorite picture:

I didn't have a good time when:

I'm looking forward to planning my next fashionista vacation to:

Fashionista's Travel Reflections

Travel Date:	**I Felt:**
Vacation Destination:	☐ energetic
Hotel/Resort/Villa:	☐ relaxed
My plans included:	☐ rested
	☐ adventurous
	☐ anxious
	☐ sexy
	☐ tired
I ate the best meal at:	☐ like a party animal
	☐ neutral
	☐ ready to return home
I felt: in my swimwear.	

I felt most adventurous when:
I felt most relaxed when:
I felt most free when:
I felt most connected to my travel companions/family when:
I winded down at the end of the day by:
I was wearing this in my favorite picture:
I didn't have a good time when:
I'm looking forward to planning my next fashionista vacation to:

Fashionista's Travel Reflections

Travel Date:	**I Felt:**
Vacation Destination:	☐ energetic
Hotel/Resort/Villa:	☐ relaxed
My plans included:	☐ rested
	☐ adventurous
	☐ anxious
	☐ sexy
	☐ tired
I ate the best meal at:	☐ like a party animal
	☐ neutral
	☐ ready to return home
I felt: in my swimwear.	

I felt most adventurous when:
I felt most relaxed when:
I felt most free when:
I felt most connected to my travel companions/family when:
I winded down at the end of the day by:
I was wearing this in my favorite picture:
I didn't have a good time when:
I'm looking forward to planning my next fashionista vacation to:

Fashionista's Travel Reflections

Travel Date:	**I Felt:**
Vacation Destination:	☐ energetic
Hotel/Resort/Villa:	☐ relaxed
My plans included:	☐ rested
	☐ adventurous
	☐ anxious
	☐ sexy
	☐ tired
I ate the best meal at:	☐ like a party animal
	☐ neutral
	☐ ready to return home
I felt: in my swimwear.	

I felt most adventurous when:

I felt most relaxed when:

I felt most free when:

I felt most connected to my travel companions/family when:

I winded down at the end of the day by:

I was wearing this in my favorite picture:

I didn't have a good time when:

I'm looking forward to planning my next fashionista vacation to:

Fashionista's Travel Reflections

Travel Date:	**I Felt:**
Vacation Destination:	☐ energetic
Hotel/Resort/Villa:	☐ relaxed
My plans included:	☐ rested
	☐ adventurous
	☐ anxious
	☐ sexy
	☐ tired
I ate the best meal at:	☐ like a party animal
	☐ neutral
	☐ ready to return home
I felt: _____ in my swimwear.	

I felt most adventurous when:

I felt most relaxed when:

I felt most free when:

I felt most connected to my travel companions/family when:

I winded down at the end of the day by:

I was wearing this in my favorite picture:

I didn't have a good time when:

I'm looking forward to planning my next fashionista vacation to:

Fashionista's Travel Reflections

Travel Date:	I Felt:
Vacation Destination:	☐ energetic
Hotel/Resort/Villa:	☐ relaxed
My plans included:	☐ rested
	☐ adventurous
	☐ anxious
	☐ sexy
	☐ tired
I ate the best meal at:	☐ like a party animal
	☐ neutral
	☐ ready to return home
I felt: in my swimwear.	

I felt most adventurous when:

I felt most relaxed when:

I felt most free when:

I felt most connected to my travel companions/family when:

I winded down at the end of the day by:

I was wearing this in my favorite picture:

I didn't have a good time when:

I'm looking forward to planning my next fashionista vacation to:

Fashionista's Travel Reflections

Travel Date:	**I Felt:**
Vacation Destination:	☐ energetic
Hotel/Resort/Villa:	☐ relaxed
My plans included:	☐ rested
	☐ adventurous
	☐ anxious
	☐ sexy
	☐ tired
I ate the best meal at:	☐ like a party animal
	☐ neutral
	☐ ready to return home
I felt: _____ in my swimwear.	

I felt most adventurous when:

I felt most relaxed when:

I felt most free when:

I felt most connected to my travel companions/family when:

I winded down at the end of the day by:

I was wearing this in my favorite picture:

I didn't have a good time when:

I'm looking forward to planning my next fashionista vacation to:

Fashionista's Travel Reflections

Travel Date:	**I Felt:**
Vacation Destination:	☐ energetic
Hotel/Resort/Villa:	☐ relaxed
My plans included:	☐ rested
	☐ adventurous
	☐ anxious
	☐ sexy
	☐ tired
I ate the best meal at:	☐ like a party animal
	☐ neutral
	☐ ready to return home
I felt: _____ in my swimwear.	

I felt most adventurous when:

I felt most relaxed when:

I felt most free when:

I felt most connected to my travel companions/family when:

I winded down at the end of the day by:

I was wearing this in my favorite picture:

I didn't have a good time when:

I'm looking forward to planning my next fashionista vacation to:

Fashionista's Travel Reflections

Travel Date:	**I Felt:**
Vacation Destination:	☐ energetic
Hotel/Resort/Villa:	☐ relaxed
My plans included:	☐ rested
	☐ adventurous
	☐ anxious
	☐ sexy
	☐ tired
I ate the best meal at:	☐ like a party animal
	☐ neutral
	☐ ready to return home
I felt: _____ in my swimwear.	

I felt most adventurous when:

I felt most relaxed when:

I felt most free when:

I felt most connected to my travel companions/family when:

I winded down at the end of the day by:

I was wearing this in my favorite picture:

I didn't have a good time when:

I'm looking forward to planning my next fashionista vacation to:

Fashionista's Travel Reflections

Travel Date:	**I Felt:**
Vacation Destination:	☐ energetic
Hotel/Resort/Villa:	☐ relaxed
My plans included:	☐ rested
	☐ adventurous
	☐ anxious
	☐ sexy
	☐ tired
I ate the best meal at:	☐ like a party animal
	☐ neutral
	☐ ready to return home
I felt: _____ in my swimwear.	

I felt most adventurous when:

I felt most relaxed when:

I felt most free when:

I felt most connected to my travel companions/family when:

I winded down at the end of the day by:

I was wearing this in my favorite picture:

I didn't have a good time when:

I'm looking forward to planning my next fashionista vacation to:

Fashionista's Travel Reflections

Travel Date:	**I Felt:**
Vacation Destination:	☐ energetic
Hotel/Resort/Villa:	☐ relaxed
My plans included:	☐ rested
	☐ adventurous
	☐ anxious
	☐ sexy
	☐ tired
I ate the best meal at:	☐ like a party animal
	☐ neutral
	☐ ready to return home
I felt: in my swimwear.	

I felt most adventurous when:

I felt most relaxed when:

I felt most free when:

I felt most connected to my travel companions/family when:

I winded down at the end of the day by:

I was wearing this in my favorite picture:

I didn't have a good time when:

I'm looking forward to planning my next fashionista vacation to:

Fashionista's Travel Reflections

Travel Date:	**I Felt:**
Vacation Destination:	☐ energetic
Hotel/Resort/Villa:	☐ relaxed
My plans included:	☐ rested
	☐ adventurous
	☐ anxious
	☐ sexy
	☐ tired
I ate the best meal at:	☐ like a party animal
	☐ neutral
	☐ ready to return home
I felt: _____ in my swimwear.	

I felt most adventurous when:

I felt most relaxed when:

I felt most free when:

I felt most connected to my travel companions/family when:

I winded down at the end of the day by:

I was wearing this in my favorite picture:

I didn't have a good time when:

I'm looking forward to planning my next fashionista vacation to:

Fashionista's Travel Reflections

Travel Date:	**I Felt:**
Vacation Destination:	☐ energetic
Hotel/Resort/Villa:	☐ relaxed
My plans included:	☐ rested
	☐ adventurous
	☐ anxious
	☐ sexy
	☐ tired
I ate the best meal at:	☐ like a party animal
	☐ neutral
	☐ ready to return home
I felt: in my swimwear.	

I felt most adventurous when:

I felt most relaxed when:

I felt most free when:

I felt most connected to my travel companions/family when:

I winded down at the end of the day by:

I was wearing this in my favorite picture:

I didn't have a good time when:

I'm looking forward to planning my next fashionista vacation to:

Fashionista's Travel Reflections

Travel Date:	**I Felt:**
Vacation Destination:	☐ energetic
Hotel/Resort/Villa:	☐ relaxed
My plans included:	☐ rested
	☐ adventurous
	☐ anxious
	☐ sexy
	☐ tired
I ate the best meal at:	☐ like a party animal
	☐ neutral
	☐ ready to return home
I felt: in my swimwear.	

I felt most adventurous when:

I felt most relaxed when:

I felt most free when:

I felt most connected to my travel companions/family when:

I winded down at the end of the day by:

I was wearing this in my favorite picture:

I didn't have a good time when:

I'm looking forward to planning my next fashionista vacation to:

Fashionista's Travel Reflections

Travel Date:	**I Felt:**
Vacation Destination:	☐ energetic
Hotel/Resort/Villa:	☐ relaxed
My plans included:	☐ rested
	☐ adventurous
	☐ anxious
	☐ sexy
	☐ tired
I ate the best meal at:	☐ like a party animal
	☐ neutral
	☐ ready to return home
I felt: _____ in my swimwear.	

I felt most adventurous when:

I felt most relaxed when:

I felt most free when:

I felt most connected to my travel companions/family when:

I winded down at the end of the day by:

I was wearing this in my favorite picture:

I didn't have a good time when:

I'm looking forward to planning my next fashionista vacation to:

Fashionista's Travel Reflections

Travel Date:	**I Felt:**
Vacation Destination:	☐ energetic
Hotel/Resort/Villa:	☐ relaxed
My plans included:	☐ rested
	☐ adventurous
	☐ anxious
	☐ sexy
	☐ tired
I ate the best meal at:	☐ like a party animal
	☐ neutral
	☐ ready to return home
I felt: in my swimwear.	

I felt most adventurous when:
I felt most relaxed when:
I felt most free when:
I felt most connected to my travel companions/family when:
I winded down at the end of the day by:
I was wearing this in my favorite picture:
I didn't have a good time when:
I'm looking forward to planning my next fashionista vacation to:

Fashionista's Travel Reflections

Travel Date:	**I Felt:**
Vacation Destination:	☐ energetic
Hotel/Resort/Villa:	☐ relaxed
My plans included:	☐ rested
	☐ adventurous
	☐ anxious
	☐ sexy
	☐ tired
I ate the best meal at:	☐ like a party animal
	☐ neutral
	☐ ready to return home
I felt: in my swimwear.	

I felt most adventurous when:

I felt most relaxed when:

I felt most free when:

I felt most connected to my travel companions/family when:

I winded down at the end of the day by:

I was wearing this in my favorite picture:

I didn't have a good time when:

I'm looking forward to planning my next fashionista vacation to:

Fashionista's Travel Reflections

Travel Date:	**I Felt:**
Vacation Destination:	☐ energetic
Hotel/Resort/Villa:	☐ relaxed
My plans included:	☐ rested
	☐ adventurous
	☐ anxious
	☐ sexy
	☐ tired
I ate the best meal at:	☐ like a party animal
	☐ neutral
	☐ ready to return home
I felt: _____ in my swimwear.	

I felt most adventurous when:

I felt most relaxed when:

I felt most free when:

I felt most connected to my travel companions/family when:

I winded down at the end of the day by:

I was wearing this in my favorite picture:

I didn't have a good time when:

I'm looking forward to planning my next fashionista vacation to:

Fashionista's Travel Reflections

Travel Date:	**I Felt:**
Vacation Destination:	☐ energetic
Hotel/Resort/Villa:	☐ relaxed
My plans included:	☐ rested
	☐ adventurous
	☐ anxious
	☐ sexy
	☐ tired
I ate the best meal at:	☐ like a party animal
	☐ neutral
	☐ ready to return home
I felt: in my swimwear.	

I felt most adventurous when:
I felt most relaxed when:
I felt most free when:
I felt most connected to my travel companions/family when:
I winded down at the end of the day by:
I was wearing this in my favorite picture:
I didn't have a good time when:
I'm looking forward to planning my next fashionista vacation to:

Fashionista's Travel Reflections

Travel Date:	**I Felt:**
Vacation Destination:	☐ energetic
Hotel/Resort/Villa:	☐ relaxed
My plans included:	☐ rested
	☐ adventurous
	☐ anxious
	☐ sexy
	☐ tired
I ate the best meal at:	☐ like a party animal
	☐ neutral
	☐ ready to return home
I felt: in my swimwear.	

I felt most adventurous when:
I felt most relaxed when:
I felt most free when:
I felt most connected to my travel companions/family when:
I winded down at the end of the day by:
I was wearing this in my favorite picture:
I didn't have a good time when:
I'm looking forward to planning my next fashionista vacation to:

Fashionista's Travel Reflections

Travel Date:	**I Felt:**
Vacation Destination:	☐ energetic
Hotel/Resort/Villa:	☐ relaxed
My plans included:	☐ rested
	☐ adventurous
	☐ anxious
	☐ sexy
	☐ tired
I ate the best meal at:	☐ like a party animal
	☐ neutral
	☐ ready to return home
I felt: in my swimwear.	

I felt most adventurous when:
I felt most relaxed when:
I felt most free when:
I felt most connected to my travel companions/family when:
I winded down at the end of the day by:
I was wearing this in my favorite picture:
I didn't have a good time when:
I'm looking forward to planning my next fashionista vacation to:

Fashionista's Travel Reflections

Travel Date:	**I Felt:**
Vacation Destination:	☐ energetic
Hotel/Resort/Villa:	☐ relaxed
My plans included:	☐ rested
	☐ adventurous
	☐ anxious
	☐ sexy
	☐ tired
I ate the best meal at:	☐ like a party animal
	☐ neutral
	☐ ready to return home
I felt: in my swimwear.	

I felt most adventurous when:

I felt most relaxed when:

I felt most free when:

I felt most connected to my travel companions/family when:

I winded down at the end of the day by:

I was wearing this in my favorite picture:

I didn't have a good time when:

I'm looking forward to planning my next fashionista vacation to:

Fashionista's Travel Reflections

Travel Date:	**I Felt:**
Vacation Destination:	☐ energetic
Hotel/Resort/Villa:	☐ relaxed
My plans included:	☐ rested
	☐ adventurous
	☐ anxious
	☐ sexy
	☐ tired
I ate the best meal at:	☐ like a party animal
	☐ neutral
	☐ ready to return home
I felt: in my swimwear.	

I felt most adventurous when:
I felt most relaxed when:
I felt most free when:
I felt most connected to my travel companions/family when:
I winded down at the end of the day by:
I was wearing this in my favorite picture:
I didn't have a good time when:
I'm looking forward to planning my next fashionista vacation to:

My Thoughts & Feelings Matter

My Thoughts & Feelings Matter

My Thoughts & Feelings Matter

My Thoughts & Feelings Matter

My Thoughts & Feelings Matter

Kinyatta E. Gray is a published author and the CEO of FlightsInStilettos, LLC.

She's also the Chief Beach Towel Designer of FlightsInStilettos Glam Girl Beach Towels.

Websites:
FlightsInStilettos.com and **KinyattaGray.com**

Travel is glamorous only in retrospect.

~Paul Theroux

www.ingramcontent.com/pod-product-compliance
Lightning Source LLC
Chambersburg PA
CBHW042342300426
44109CB00048B/2673